FUN FACT FILE: EARTH SCIENCE

20 FUN FACTS ABOUT EARTH'S RESOURCES

By Sarah Machajewski

Gareth Stevens PUBLISHING

Please visit our website, www.garethstevens.com. For a free color catalog of all our high-quality books, call toll free 1-800-542-2595 or fax 1-877-542-2596.

Cataloging-in-Publication Data

Names: Machajewski, Sarah.
Title: 20 fun facts about earth's resources / Sarah Machajewski.
Description: New York : Gareth Stevens Publishing, 2018. | Series: Fun fact file: earth science | Includes index.
Identifiers: ISBN 9781538211779 (pbk.) | ISBN 9781538211793 (library bound) | ISBN 9781538211786 (6 pack)
Subjects: LCSH: Natural resources–Juvenile literature.
Classification: LCC HC85.M33 2018 | DDC 333.7–dc23

First Edition

Published in 2018 by
Gareth Stevens Publishing
111 East 14th Street, Suite 349
New York, NY 10003

Designer: Sam DeMartin
Editor: Joan Stoltman

Photo credits: Cover, p. 1 Richard Cavalleri/Shutterstock.com; p. 5 asiseeit/E+/Getty Images; p. 6 Natthapong Ponepormmarat/Shutterstock.com; p. 7 BlueRingMedia/Shutterstock.com; p. 8 jopelka/Shutterstock.com; p. 9 Merkushev Vasiliy/Shutterstock.com; p. 10 zhu difeng/Shutterstock.com; p. 11 Bruce McQueen/Shutterstock.com; p. 12 Frank Röder/imageBROKER/Getty Images; p. 13 Christian Petersen-Clausen/Moment/Getty Images; p. 14 Brendan Howard/Shutterstock.com; p. 15 Rasta777/Shutterstock.com; p. 16 Branork/Wikimedia Commons; p. 17 Mikhail Mishunin/Shutterstock.com; p. 18 Fokin Oleg/Shutterstock.com; p. 19 Joe Gough/Shutterstock.com; p. 20 kram9/Shutterstock.com; p. 21 Patila/Shutterstock.com; p. 22 Monkey Business Images/Shutterstock.com; p. 23 Rich Carey/Shutterstock.com; p. 24 Tony Prince/Shutterstock.com; p. 25 Stokkete/Shutterstock.com; p. 26 Mike Pellinni/Shutterstock.com; p. 27 (coal) xtrekx/Shutterstock.com; p. 27 (oil) Mykola59/Shutterstock.com; p. 27 (wood) Shu Ba/Shutterstock.com; p. 29 Ryan M. Bolton/Shutterstock.com.

Printed in the United States of America

CPSIA compliance information: Batch #CW18GS: For further information contact Gareth Stevens, New York, New York at 1-800-542-2595.

Contents

Words in the glossary appear in **bold** type the first time they are used in the text.

Survival, Naturally

We breathe air. We drink water. We use rocks to build. These things sound simple, right? You may not realize it, but you couldn't survive on Earth without these things! In fact, the reason many places in space don't have plants or animals is because they don't have these things!

Air, water, and rocks are all natural resources. A natural resource is something found in nature that people use. Some natural resources keep us alive, like the sun's heat. Others improve our lives, like gold and other metals found in the earth.

Can you identify all the natural resources in this picture?

Our Sun!

Heat and light are forms of **energy**. Energy from the sun is called solar energy. Plants, animals, and people need it to stay alive.

FACT 1

It takes sunlight 8 minutes to reach Earth!

The sunlight you see is actually 8 minutes old! Without the light and heat from the sun, Earth would be a cold, dark, lifeless place. Most forms of life need sunlight to survive!

FACT 2

Sunlight is food—for plants!

Just like us, plants need energy to live. But they don't get energy from food like we do! Plants get their energy from sunlight and use it in a **process** called photosynthesis.

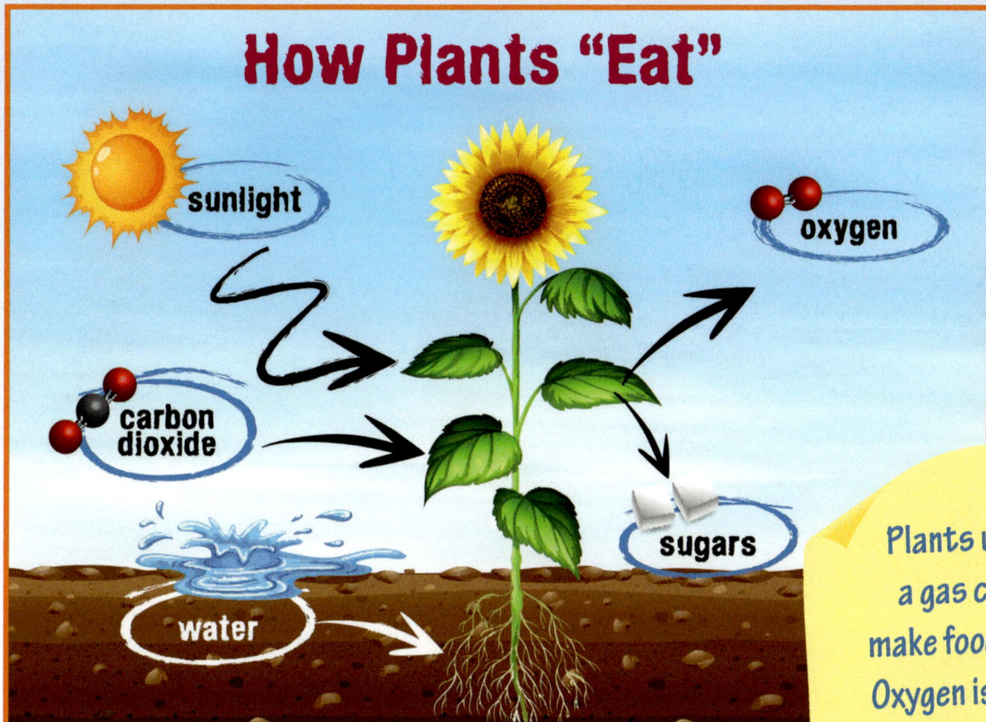

Plants use sunlight, water, and a gas called carbon dioxide to make food during photosynthesis. Oxygen is a waste gas that plants give off during photosynthesis. All animals need oxygen to live!

FACT 3

Earth has the same amount of water today that it did when the planet was formed!

New water is never created, and water is never lost. Instead, water is always moving through a cycle, or chain of steps, called the water cycle.

The Water Cycle

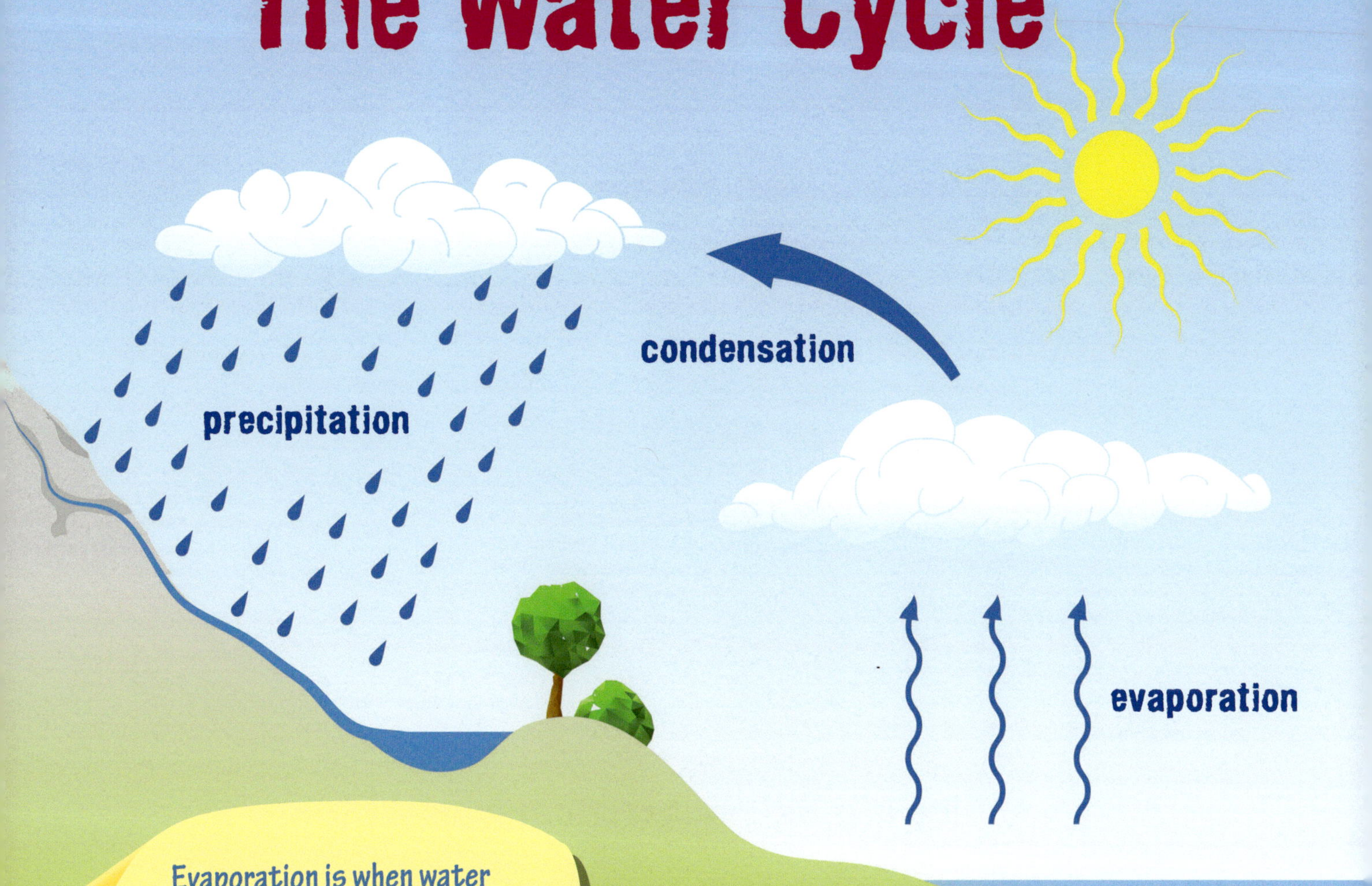

Evaporation is when water changes from a liquid to a gas. Condensation is when a gas cools and becomes liquid. Precipitation is when water, as a solid or liquid, is so heavy that it falls out of the sky!

Wind and Air

A turbine is a machine that creates power as it spins. Wind turbine blades are pushed into spinning by wind.

FACT 4

Wind turbines can be as big as the Statue of Liberty!

A wind turbine is a big machine that turns wind into power. It can be more than 260 feet (79 m) tall. The blade of a wind turbine can be over 160 feet (49 m) long.

FACT 6

Wind passing over one wind turbine can power about 500 homes.

Wind is an important **source** of energy because it doesn't create **pollution**. Wind is also free, and it will never run out. So wind energy is good for Earth!

Scientists think wind power will supply about 35 percent of the energy used by people by 2050.

FACT 6

Fossil fuels began forming when dinosaurs roamed Earth!

As the name suggests, "fossil fuels" are really old—perhaps even 300 million years old! These sources of energy are made up of broken down remains from organisms that lived long ago. Organisms are living creatures, such as plants and animals.

Fossil fuels are found inside Earth's crust. It can be very expensive—and harmful to nature—to get fossil fuels out of the earth.

Many scientists are concerned about how fast we're using fossil fuels and how it will affect the future of the planet. Once we use up our fossil fuels, they're gone forever.

FACT 7

Over 80 percent of the energy we use is supplied by fossil fuels.

Fossil fuels provide us with the fuels that power cars, trucks, buses, boats, and planes. In homes, heat and electricity often come from fossil fuels.

Coal takes a very long time to form, and we're using it faster than it forms. No one's sure how long our country's coal supply will last—it could be anywhere from 110 to 235 years!

FACT 8

Coal takes hundreds of millions of years to form.

Coal comes from plants that lived hundreds of millions of years ago. After the plants died, **layers** of **sediment**, dirt, and rocks slowly covered them. Over time, heat and weight turned the plants into coal. Today, coal contains all the energy of those ancient plants.

FACT 9

Coal was discovered in China nearly 4,000 years ago.

People who've studied history think this was the first time people burned a fossil fuel. Since then, coal has become one of the most used natural resources. This black "rock" is used all over the world as a source of heat and electricity.

Coal supplies about 30 percent of the electricity in the United States. The United States is the second-largest coal producer in the world.

FACT 10

Oil is a thick, gooey liquid made of plant and animal remains.

Oil is also called petroleum. It's made when **organic** matter piles up at the bottom of oceans and rivers and slowly changes over millions of years.

Natural petroleum can be yellow or black in color. The word "petroleum" comes from Latin words meaning "rock oil."

FACT 11

Oil is found deep within layers of rocks.

Oil companies remove oil from the ground by digging deep wells. The oil is pumped out and carried away through big pipes or on ships. Factories called refineries turn the oil into gasoline. Gasoline is the liquid fuel for cars, trucks, and boats.

FACT 12

About 6 percent of Earth's crust is made of iron.

Iron is an element that's found all over the planet—and deep inside it! Rocks that have iron are called iron ore. They can be rusty red, yellow, purple, or black.

This may look like a simple rock, but its colors reveal an important clue: It has iron. This is no regular rock!

FACT 13

Iron is used to make steel, one of the strongest things to build with.

Steel is a very strong metal that lasts for many years. It's used to make machines, tools, cars, trucks, buildings (including **skyscrapers**), and more. About 98 percent of iron ore taken from the earth is used to make steel!

Steel is a widely used building **material**. It's one of the big reasons cities can grow so large today!

Super Soil

It's important to take care of our soil, as it takes care of the things we need to survive.

FACT 14

The ground beneath our feet isn't just dirt—it's a living, breathing home.

Full of important **nutrients** and **minerals**, soil is necessary for all kinds of life. It **filters** our water and stores gases that we need to breathe. Healthy soil produces healthy, strong plants.

FACT 15

Worms keep the soil healthy!

Worms are very important. They create air pockets and put important nutrients back into the soil. Soil that contains a lot of worms is very healthy.

Many gardeners introduce worms into their garden beds to help their plants!

FACT 16

Wood is used to make about 10,000 things we use—from paper to furniture to houses.

Wood is an important building material. For hundreds of years, people have been cutting down trees to use them for building and making tools that help us live.

A carpenter is a person who builds with and creates objects from wood. Being a carpenter requires training and talent!

Every minute, an area of rainforest the size of 36 football fields is cut down. If we lose these trees, it will have a huge effect on Earth! It's important to help save the rainforests.

FACT 17

Rainforests only cover about 6 percent of Earth's surface, but they're very important!

Rainforests keep our water and air supplies healthy and clean. They control Earth's weather patterns. They're home to over half the world's animal **species** and two-thirds of its plant species.

Weaving is the practice of forming threads into material. People all over the world have traditionally used weaving to create clothes, blankets, and more.

FACT 18

Most of your clothing is made of plants!

Cotton and linen are both materials that come from plants. Their fibers are gathered and used to make shirts, pants, dresses, shorts, and more. Today, cotton is the plant that's most used to make clothes.

FACT 19

Plants give us everything we need to survive, such as food and oxygen.

People have even been using plants to treat illnesses and make pain go away for thousands of years.

Many flowers have also been used to help people. These flowers are often still used in ways that were discovered thousands of years ago!

Many, Many Resources

Rivers are an important resource. Because rivers supply water, cities were often built near them. They played an important role in travel and trade.

FACT 20

People can use only about 1 percent of Earth's water.

Almost 97 percent of Earth's water is salt water. The rest is freshwater, or water that doesn't have salt. Around 2 percent of freshwater is locked in glaciers and ice caps. The rest is for us to use for everything from drinking and bathing to cooking and cleaning!

Renewable Resources vs. Nonrenewable Resources

renewable resources	nonrenewable resources
wind	metals
sun	fossil fuels
water	coal
wood	uranium
	natural gas
	oil

Natural resources can be either renewable or nonrenewable. A renewable resource is one that won't ever get used up. When there is only a certain amount of a resource to use, it's called a nonrenewable resource.

Protect the Planet

Earth's resources help our lives and improve our living conditions. Whether they're renewable or not, resources are necessary for survival!

When we think about our planet's resources, it's important to remember that it's not just people who use them. We share our planet with plants and animals that need these resources to survive, too! It's important to protect our natural resources. If we don't, we risk destroying the planet we all call home.

Is it fair that people have cut down the rainforests that are home to these animals?

Glossary

energy: power used to do work

filter: to collect bits from a liquid passing through

layer: one thickness of something lying over or under another

material: something used to make something

mineral: matter important in small quantities for the nutrition of animals

nutrient: something a living thing needs to grow and stay alive

organic: having to do with living things

pollution: the act of polluting or the state of being polluted

process: a series of actions that produce something

sediment: matter that sinks to the bottom of a liquid

skyscraper: a very tall building with many floors

source: the cause or starting point of something

species: kinds

For More Information

Books

Grady, Colin. *Fossil Fuels*. New York, NY: Enslow Publishing, 2017.

Loria, Laura. *What Are Resources?* New York, NY: Britannica Educational Publishing, 2017.

Sherman, Jill. *Fertile Land and Soil*. New York, NY: Enslow Publishing, 2017.

Websites

Energy Kids: Energy Sources
www.eia.gov/kids/energy.cfm?page=2
The US Energy Information Administration provides a resource to help kids learn about energy resources.

The Story of Fossil Fuels
climatekids.nasa.gov/fossil-fuels-coal/
In NASA's Climate Kids series, readers learn about fossil fuels.

The Water Cycle - USGS Water Science School
water.usgs.gov/edu/watercycle-kids-beg.html
Learn about the water cycle with this fun diagram.

Index